THE TET OFFENSIVE

Below: **Machine gunner defends Khe Sanh.**

Previous page: **Machine gunner walks through the rubble of Cholon outside Saigon.**

THE TET OFFENSIVE
January–April, 1968

Tracey Burke
and
Mimi Gleason

GALLERY BOOKS
An imprint of W. H. Smith Publishers, Inc.
112 Madison Avenue
New York City 10016

Library of Congress Cataloging-in-Publication Data

Burke, Tracey.
  The Tet offensive, January-April 1968 / Tracey Burke and Mimi
Gleason
    184p. 48x62 cm.
    ISBN 0-8317-8696-5
    1. Tet Offensive, 1968.   I. Gleason, Mimi   II. Title.
DS557.8.T4B87 1988   88-11155
959.704'3 – dc 19   CIP

This 1988 edition published by Gallery Books,
an imprint of W. H. Smith, Publishers, Inc.
112 Madison Avenue, New York, NY 10016

Prepared by Combined Books
26 Summit Grove, Suite 207
Bryn Mawr, PA 19010

Project Director: Robert L. Pigeon
Project Coordinator: Antoinette Bauer

Produced by Wieser and Wieser, Inc.
118 East 25th Street, New York, NY 10010

CONTENTS

Fighting extends around BOQ #3 in Saigon on the first day of the Tet Offensive.

C-130 delivers supplies to the besieged camp at Khe Sanh. A cable attaches to the ground pulling cargo from the plane as plane flies low to ground.

Vietnam in 1967

The 1968 Tet Offensive has been called the turning point of the Vietnam War. It was the first extensive effort by the North Vietnamese and the Viet Cong against South Vietnam and the United States, which had been there several years in support of the South Vietnamese government. Officially the Tet Offensive was from January 30 to April 1. American public opinion and national policy changed dramatically after Tet, leading to the gradual withdrawal of American troops from Vietnam.

The Tet holiday was the most sacred and important time of year for Vietnamese of all beliefs and social classes in both North and South Vietnam. It was the lunar new year which marked the beginning of spring and usually occurred at the end of January or beginning of February. It was described to Americans stationed in South Vietnam during the war as "a combination All Souls' Day, a family celebration, a spring festival, a national holiday, and an overall manifestation of a way of life." The Tet celebration lasted seven days, of which the first three were the most important. It began with the veneration of the family shrine and public worship and also included feasts, visits, and jubilant public festivals.

Vietnam was a narrow strip of land that was split into two countries at the 17th parallel during the 1954 Geneva Conference that concluded the Indochina War against the French. North Vietnam, also known as the Democratic Republic of Vietnam, was placed under the control of the Communist Viet Minh led by Ho Chi Minh. It was bordered in the north by China, in the west by Laos, and in the east by the Gulf of Tonkin; its capital city was Hanoi. South Vietnam, or the Republic of Vietnam, was left in the hands of the ancestral emperor, Bao Dai, and his prime minister, Ngo Dinh Diem. It was surrounded by Laos and Cambodia to the west, the Gulf of Thailand to the southwest, and the South China Sea to the east and southeast; its capital city was Saigon.

The National Liberation Front (NLF), or Viet Cong (VC), was an organization of South Vietnamese nationalists who wished to reunite North and South Vietnam. It was formed by members of the Saigon elite who believed in the right of people to choose their own form of government and not to have a leader imposed on them by outsiders. The NLF began as a political organization, but became more militant as its members realized they would need the support of the Communist North Vietnamese in order to achieve their goals.

In July 1967 leaders in Hanoi decided to stage an offensive against the American and South Vietnamese forces in the cities throughout South Vietnam. The North Vietnamese Army and Viet Cong (NVA/VC) hoped to drain American resources and commitment to the war. However, the United States, far from pulling out of South Vietnam, similarly intended to wear down North Vietnamese commitment to the war and by 1967 had substantially increased its forces. At the same time, the VC were losing resources and refuge in the countryside as many people moved to the city to avoid the destruction of the war. Consequently, many VC soldiers were deserting to join their families.

The most ambitious goal of the planned offensive was for the South Vietnamese people to join the uprising and for the Army of the Republic of Vietnam (ARVN) to be permanently broken. The more realistic and ultimately more obtainable goals included: eliminating the immunity of civilians in the cities from the effects of the war, increasing the number of refugees to further strain the weak economy of South Vietnam, straining the relations between South Vietnam and the United States, heightening US casualty rates, and generating greater opposition to the war in the United States. In short, the North Vietnamese and Viet Cong hoped to win a military, political, and psychological victory that would destroy support for Nguyen Van Thieu, president of South Vietnam, and for the war itself among the American people and Congress by shifting from a prolonged war strategy to a "general offensive—general uprising." A lame South Vietnamese government and army, along with pressure from home, would force the United States to negotiate for peace and accept compromise.

The North Vietnamese and Viet Cong leaders started planning for the offensive in July 1967. They intended to complement conventional army warfare with guerrilla tactics to seize important targets, to limit the ability of American and South Vietnamese troops in the cities to fight back, and to prevent reinforcements from getting into the cities. New recruits trained for various missions; veterans, and supplies were transported from the north. The Viet Cong, in an attempt to gain broader appeal among the people, announced on its Liberation Radio its commitment to civil freedoms such as speech, assembly, and elections.

In the fall of 1967 North Vietnamese/Viet Cong troops engaged detachments from the Army of the Republic of Vietnam and the U.S. Armed Forces (ARVN/USAF) in "border battles" at Con Thien near the Demilitarized Zone (DMZ), Dak To in the central highlands, and Loc Ninh near the Cambodian border. These campaigns were undertaken to draw American interest and resources to the border regions and leave the defending South Vietnamese and American troops in the cities spread too thinly to repulse the major thrust of the attack. They also hid North Vietnamese movement into the south and provided an opportunity to better coordinate the regular army and guerrilla forces before the planned nationwide offensive began.

As a sign of unity with South Vietnamese allies during the Tet Offensive, some North Vietnamese soldiers wore armbands emblazened with "Born in the North, Died in the

Aerial view of Hue, the ancient capital of Vietnam, before the attack. Looking south at the city, the Perfume River is visible in the background. The Citadel and ancient wall can also be seen.

Infantryman at Khe Sanh compares the lighter Chinese 60mm mortar gun to the heavier but more accurate US model.

South."

By early 1968, the American press and Congress sensed a lack of support for the USAF in Vietnam. Yet, the President and most of his advisers were still optimistic about US chances for success, though "success" remained undefined. Of all those who had access to the President, only Secretary of Defense Robert McNamara was critical of the war policy. As early as October 1966, he tried to convince President Lyndon B. Johnson to limit the bombing of North Vietnam and to attempt to work out a political settlement. McNamara originally favored bombing the North and believed the war could bring the VC under control. After personally going to Vietnam and examining the results of American tactics, however, he could see no significant evidence that bombing hampered the North Vietnamese's ability to continue the war; in fact, the indiscriminate destruction added to the ill feelings of the villagers towards the Americans.

In a May 1967 memo to the President, McNamara wrote: The time has come for us to eliminate the ambiguities from our minimum objectives—our commitments—in Vietnam. Specifically, two principles must be articulated, and policies and actions brought in line with them: (1) Our commitment is only to see that the people of South Vietnam are permitted to determine their own future. (2) This commitment ceases if the country ceases to help itself.

It follows that no matter how much we might hope for some things, our commitment is not:

. . . to ensure that a particular person or group remains in power, nor that the power runs to every corner of the land (though we prefer certain types and we hope their writ will run throughout Vietnam),

To guarantee that the self-chosen government is non-Communist (though we believe and strongly hope it will be), and

To insist that the independent South Vietnam remain separate from North Vietnam (though in the short run we would prefer it that way).

McNamara's new dovish attitude led to dissension within the administration and rumors of his leaving. In May and August, when these rumors abounded, there was conflict in the White House about the decision to bomb North Vietnam. In May, McNamara wanted Johnson to reduce the bombing, while the military authorities wanted to expand the war effort. General Earle G. Wheeler, chairman of the Joint Chiefs of Staff, argued that a reduction in bombing would lead to an "aerial Dien Bien Phu," which took place in 1954, but was of such great significance that it was still in the minds of the military more than a decade later. In the Dien Bien Phu valley in North Vietnam Ho Chi Minh's Vietminh defeated the French, who had grievously underestimated the strength of the guerrilla cause, and were overconfident in their own superiority. Both sides had wanted a decisive victory to strengthen their diplomatic position before upcoming Geneva Conference peace talks. The French commander, General Henri Navarre, believed that once he engaged the guerrillas in a conventional battle, he would be able to quickly overpower them with France's superior military. He established French control in the valley and on the airstrip by assembling a large airborne force and fortifying the position. Navarre underestimated General Vo Nguyen Giap's ability to transport masses of troops over long distances and to effectively plan for an operation of the extent necessary. By the start of the confrontation on March 13, Vietminh soldiers outnumbered the French by a five to one ratio. The French were also surprised to find that the Vietminh possessed both howitzers capable of shooting down planes and camouflage capable of protecting their position from French planes that survived the artillery barrage. This was indeed a threat to the French who depended on aircraft support for supplies and evacuation of the wounded. By May 7, the day before the Geneva Conference started, air support had become extremely unreliable due to poor visibility caused by spring rains coupled with the Vietminh's ability to quickly knock out two of the three French artillery bases. The Vietminh had succeeded in constructing an intricate web of trenches around the French installation which enabled the Vietminh to dynamite the French camp from underground—a resounding defeat by the Vietnamese was the eventual result. The French still had the military capability to continue the war, but after so much propaganda about French strength and Vietnamese weakness, the humiliation at Dien Bien Phu convinced the French people that they could not win the war and they no longer had the will to continue the struggle.

So in August of 1967, with the ambitious General Giap still in evidence, there was considerable military backing when the President ignored McNamara's advice and increased the bombing. In September, the Secretary wanted the US to encourage Saigon to accept a coalition government that included non-Communist members of the NLF.

That same summer, Assistant Secretary of State William Bundy also criticized American strategy in Vietnam. He disagreed with the proposal to send ground troops into North Vietnam because of the possibility of China's intervention and, along with the CIA, warned of the threat of Soviet intervention if the US bombed North Vietnam's harbors.

On November 2, 1967, Johnson met with his "Wise Men," influential people whose advice the President occasionally sought about foreign policy. Almost unanimously, they approved US strategy and believed the public should have the opportunity to fully appreciate the progress that the United States was making in South Vietnam. Johnson did not arrange to have McNamara's arguments presented at the meeting. On November 28, President Johnson nominated McNamara as president of the World Bank, and Clark Clifford took over as Secretary of Defense.

Johnson continued to receive different versions of the situation in Vietnam and chose to believe the more optimistic of them. He disregarded the unsettling reports concerning US strategy by the CIA and the Pentagon Offices of International Security Affairs and Systems Analysis. He

also ignored the bombing study from McNamara which said that the bombing of Hanoi had not adversely affected the military strength of the North Vietnamese or the Viet Cong in the South. Johnson instead relied on more optimistic descriptions of the war which could be used to soothe the public's increasing opposition. General William C. Westmoreland, head of Military Assistance Command, Vietnam (MACV), told the President that the bombings had successfully wounded the enemy forces and the North Vietnamese/Viet Cong had become weaker in the cities in 1967 and were being forced to turn to more reckless tactics.

The US knew almost immediately that the North Vietnamese and the Viet Cong were planning something. Back in July, senior North Vietnamese diplomats from around the world had been called home to Hanoi. In November, an attack order was captured which read that the "time has come for direct revolution and that the opportunity for a general offensive and general uprising is within reach." The center of military command located in Saigon ignored the order because it was believed to be propaganda intended to boost North Vietnamese/Viet Cong morale. The captured information was released to the press on January 5, 1968, but still failed to evoke much of a reaction.

In December 1967, MACV had received reports of extensive troop movement throughout the country, especially towards Saigon, Da Nang, Hue, Khe Sanh, the DMZ, and a number of provincial and district capitals. At the same time, the US Army reported an increase in the number of terrorist incidents and a greater amount of contact with the enemy. General Wheeler and President Johnson both predicted offensive maneuvers by the NVA/VC. Westmoreland stated that the enemy might "undertake an intensified countrywide effort, perhaps a maximum effort, over a relatively short period." On January 4, 1968, the US 4th Infantry Division detected evidence that Pleiku, a provincial town in the middle of South Vietnam, would be attacked prior to the Tet holidays. Later in the month, South Vietnamese soldiers captured similar information. And on January 28, South Vietnamese agents discovered Viet Cong encouraging people in Qui Nhon, a central coastal town, to support the uprising, to depose President Nguyen Van Thieu's government, and to join the people of Saigon, Hue, and other cities who had already been "liberated." American and South Vietnamese officials also noticed fewer recent enemy defections indicating high morale in the North Vietnamese/Viet Cong camp.

The United States and South Vietnam knew an attack was imminent, but by misinterpreting intelligence, they misjudged the scope and intensity of the attack. Through the fall of 1967, Military Assistance Command underestimated North Vietnamese/ Viet Cong size and fire power. Erroneous information led not only American military officials, but also Congress and the American people, to believe that the ARVN/ USAF were winning and that the NVA/VC were not capable of holding their own in conventional warfare.

That November, LBJ had Westmoreland and Ambassador Ellsworth Bunker return to Washington from Saigon to report on the situation in South Vietnam. Both men stressed to Congress and to the press that progress was being made. Westmoreland was optimistic about the military aspects of the war but was not as confident as the President about the stability of the South Vietnamese government. The general had decided that Thieu's government did not have enough popular support and was corrupt. Westmoreland's and Bunker's statements, coupled with Johnson's positive outlook, strengthened the hope that the end of the war was approaching.

Westmoreland expected an aggressive move by the North Vietnamese/Viet Cong before or after Tet, but, despite some obvious signs, he did not expect it on the holiday itself. However, 1968 was not the first year in which the Vietnamese launched an offensive on an important holiday. The Vietnamese folk hero Quang Trung led a surprise attack against the Chinese during

Tet 1789. Westmoreland had a statue of Quang Trung in his office but did not appreciate its significance. More recently (and more relevently), General Vo Nguyen Giap had led the newly formed Vietnam People's Army against French outposts on Christmas Eve 1944; in 1960, Viet Cong commandos raided the military headquarters at Tay Ninh near Saigon on Tet Eve. The US overlooked these historical precedents. Then in 1968, the North Vietnamese government announced that the Tet holiday would begin on January 29, instead of January 30, because of unique positioning of the earth, sun, and moon. In truth, they wanted the North Vietnamese civilians to be able to celebrate Tet before the anticipated American retaliatory bombings. The US failed to notice this change; its attention was focused on an attack at Khe Sanh.

The North Vietnamese and Viet Cong had granted truces on every Christmas, New Year's, and Tet since 1963. The United States upheld this practice beginning with Christmas 1965. The hostilities ceased every holiday although the US continually complained about violations of the truces.

Westmoreland did not want Thieu to declare a truce for Tet 1968. The general and Ambassador Bunker both informed Johnson that a ceasefire would not be wise in the northern provinces, the DMZ, and part of North Vietnam. Thieu insisted that the truce was necessary for the morale of the South Vietnamese Army. As a compromise, Thieu agreed to reduce the truce to 36 hours instead of the traditional 48 and to keep 50 percent of South Vietnamese soldiers on alert. He would also allow the regions about which Westmoreland was most concerned to remain on full alert, but would wait until six hours before the truce was to begin before informing the forces in those areas. However, he never made the announcement, and by the time American officials realized what was going on and called off the ceasefire, many of the soldiers had left to join their families for the holiday.

Although the Tet Offensive was so named because of the large number of cities attacked during the new year's holiday, there were several North Vietnamese/Viet Cong offensive actions in January 1968, before the 30th and 31st. The best known site of battle before Tet was the siege at Khe Sanh, a Marine post of I Corps, which began on January 22. Less is commonly known about the smaller attacks on various bases even earlier in the month. On January 3, the North Vietnamese/Viet Cong bombarded Da Nang Air Base, damaging 27 aircraft. They also attacked two artillery bases and six South Vietnamese Army posts in the area. Later that night, in an attack of the Ban Me Thuot airfield, fifteen aircraft were damaged, while the headquarters of the 1st Cavalry Division at An Khe was attacked, also sustaining damage to aircraft. Substantial confrontations continued throughout the month.

On the nights of January 30 and 31, 100,000 North Vietnamese/Viet Cong troops launched a nationwide, seemingly well-organized attack on many of South Vietnam's major cities. The Tet Offensive included 36 of the 43 provincial capitals, five of the six autonomous cities, and 64 of the 242 district capitals. Among those cities attacked were: Saigon, Quang Tri, Hue, Da Nang, Mha Trang, Qui Mhon, Kontum, Ban Me Thuot, Dalat, Phan Thiet, My Tho, Can Tho, and Ben Tre. In most of the attacks, the defending forces repelled the advances easily and quickly. The extent of the attacks genuinely surprised the military leadership, but the extensive power of the American and South Vietnamese forces overwhelmed the attackers in the provinces.

The method of attack was similar in all of the cities. Guerrillas used the holiday festivities as cover to enter the cities and to prepare weapons for the assault. Under rocket and mortar fire, troops then entered the cities and joined infiltrators or sympathizers who acted as guides.

Stockpiles of 105mm howitzer shells surround the base at Khe Sanh before the Tet Offensive began. The base at Khe Sanh had been under attack since January 21, 1968—ten days before the surprise attack on Saigon.

The 155mm howitzer was used to provide infantry fire support outside the perimeter at Khe Sanh in the days immediately preceeding the Tet Offensive.

At left: General Westmoreland reviews damage
to the embassy the day after the attack.
Although Westmoreland expected an offensive
in the early months of 1968, he never
anticipated that the attack would begin on the
Vietnamese holiday called Tet. Below:
American Embassy building in downtown
Saigon was surrounded by a cement wall, but
was not heavily guarded.

Evacuees flee homes in Hue as American troops enter the city on February 21, following the NVA and VC occupation.

Hue

The attack at Hue on I Corps was a psychological victory for the North Vietnamese/Viet Cong, for Hue was the ancestral capital of all of Vietnam and full of cultural history. With the help of the French, Emperor Gia Long had rebuilt much of the city in the nineteenth century when he reestablished his family's dynasty in Vietnam. Religious landmarks made Hue especially sacred to Buddhists. Physical destruction of the city, even by protective American firepower, could well spark anti-American sentiment, possibly enough to influence Vietnamese people in both the North and the South to support the revolution.

Hue was also important militarily as the third largest city in South Vietnam and the capital of Thua Thien Province. Hue was located ten kilometers from the seacoast and only 100 kilometers from the DMZ. At such a short distance from North Vietnam, enemy troops could easily infiltrate the city, and control of Hue would prepare the way for takeover of the two northernmost provinces of South Vietnam, Quang Tri and Thua Thien. These provinces were bordered by Laos, the South China Sea and the DMZ, and separated from the rest of South Vietnam by the Annamese Mountains.

Hue was divided by the Huong or Perfume River. The so-called New City lay south of the river, while the Old City, or the Citadel, lay on the north side. The Citadel looked, and for several weeks was, unassailable. Emperor Gia Long's legacy to his capital city was several concentric inner cities surrounded first by an inner wall of brick, then by a 20-foot thick, 30-foot high outer wall, and finally by the Perfume River and a moat completing the circle. The population of Hue, about 145,000 strong, included a majority of Buddhists who were historically anti-American; in fact, the Buddhist insurrections, which resulted in the ousting of the American puppet Diem in 1963, began in Hue. In 1968, when nationwide Communist radio asked the people of South Vietnam to support the Tet uprisings, the North Vietnamese/Viet Cong received the greatest civilian support in Hue, especially from Buddhists, students and university faculty.

Hue was less prepared for enemy attack than any other section of South Vietnam. US Military Assistance Command officials had received evidence of a plan for multi-battalion attack on Hue to occur around Tet. Westmoreland forwarded this information to the Pentagon, however, military officials in Hue never learned of Westmoreland's January 22 alert. Nor did they credit a warning from an American adviser known for his immoderate worrying that three North Vietnamese/Viet Cong battalions had moved from the mountains to the nearby lowlands. Finally, enemy radio communications picked up at the nearby Marine base at Phu Bai did not reach Hue authorities until the North Vietnamese/Viet Cong attack had begun. But the South Vietnamese Army, at least, was somewhat prepared, for on January 30, Brigadier General Ngo Quang Truong, commander of ARVN's 1st Division, heard about the early Tet attacks while he was at a flag-raising ceremony at the Emperor's Gate in the Citadel. He put his available men on duty and reinforced his headquarters.

As the North Vietnamese/Viet Cong prepared for the attack on Hue, their intelligence listed almost 200 targets for capture, varying in importance from Military Assistance Command headquarters to police stations, American homes to the house of the district chief's concubine. The time of attack was well planned. Not only were most units on reduced strength due to the holiday, but the weather limited supply and air cover operations.

In the very early morning of January 31, detachments from eight battalions of North Vietnamese/Viet Cong soldiers entered the city from the south under cover of low hanging fog. Within several hours, they, together with accomplices already in the city, accomplished all but two objectives: the capture of the Army of the Republic headquarters and the Military Assistance Command compound. Two battalions had attacked the MACV compound, a walled, former hotel on the south side of the Perfume River. The compound held only a few combat troops that night, but the 300 personnel successfully defended themselves against the first wave of attack. The second wave brought heavier arms including rockets against the compound, and one rocket hit a company of North Vietnamese. Thereafter, the attack lost its strength. Another battalion attacked General Truong's Division Headquarters in a corner of the Citadel; however, his alert had brought his officers to the base, so he was able to keep his command structure intact. Some enemy troops reached the infirmary but were soon repulsed. A fourth enemy battalion took control of the airfield, while other battalions spread out in the city and easily took over. The populace was now in control of the North Vietnamese/Viet Cong.

In Hue the NVA/VC released several thousand political prisoners and many of their soldiers captured earlier. They blocked Highway 1, a main thoroughfare into the city, and assigned new functions to various buildings; a hospital was used as a command post; a high school was turned into an armory/barracks building; and the Imperial Palace, home of several former emperors and located deep inside the Citadel, became their military headquarters.

Misinformation among the allied forces was partially responsible for the ease in overtaking Hue. For example, the 3rd Marine Division, which had successfully guarded areas of South Vietnam west of Hue, had been transferred closer to Khe Sanh. "Task Force X-Ray," the official re-

The destruction to homes in the city of Hue following the 25-day siege was severe.

placement to guard those areas, was variously broken up and given duties in addition to patrolling near Hue. The task force commander, General Foster Lahue, decided to stay at the nearby Phu Bai Marine base until his unit's orders were better organized, leaving the western roads to Hue unprotected and open to raiders.

Misinformation was responsible also for the lack of immediate reinforcements. Only one American company was originally sent to Hue as relief from Phu Bai, for Phu Bai officials thought just a few North Vietnamese/Viet Cong soldiers had penetrated the city. This one company accidentally met and combined with a platoon of four northbound American tanks, but still had to call for help almost immediately in order to penetrate the North Vietnamese guards around the city. Hours later, they and another company reached Military Assistance Command Vietnam headquarters. They first rescued trapped American personnel and then regrouped for a few days to plan their counterattack and to gather more reinforcements.

General Truong had problems with reinforcements as well. He ordered his outlying units to return to headquarters in the Citadel; however, many men fell victim to NVA/VC troops, who had largely succeeded in blocking roads to the city.

ARVN/USAF troops tried to regain the southern section of Hue for several days but failed at each attempt. When more troops were finally assembled, the ARVN/USAF prepared again to attack and to close off Viet Cong supply lines. The Americans were to fight south of the river while the ARVN regained the occupied sections of the Citadel, although this outline was not adhered to.

Weather at the time was cold and wet, hindering air support. US troops retook the New City slowly, gaining ground block by block as enemy forces were pushed back towards the Old City. On February 4, Comrade Son Lam, the North Vietnamese commander in the New City at this point, requested permission to withdraw to the Citadel. He received such permission but

was ordered on February 6 to return to the south side of the river and prevent the Americans from crossing to the Citadel. Although he knew that his troops would be destroyed, he complied with the order and changed his tactics. His plan was to keep the Americans busy and to kill as many as possible. On February 7, the Viet Cong blew up the main bridge over the Perfume River between the two sections of the city. By February 10, the US had pushed the enemy back from the New City to the Citadel, although sporadic enemy fire continued to remind the ARVN/USAF of the weak nature of the south bank's security.

South Vietnamese troops, meanwhile, had regained some of the Citadel, but more than half remained under NVA/VC control. With the New City secure, US units began an attack on areas north of the river. At dusk on February 11, Marines crossed the river in assault boats and entered the northwest corner of the Citadel while aircraft diverted some enemy fire. The commanders attempted to respect the sanctity of the ancestral capital and banned bombs and shells inside the Citadel, however, soon they realized that violent means were necessary. On the 12th, South Vietnam I Corps Commander Lieutenant General Hoang Xuan Lam, met with President Thieu and announced that necessary weapons would be allowed in the ancient city; only the Imperial Palace would be restricted.

Block by block fighting continued throughout the rest of Hue as the main assault on the Citadel walls continued for several days. South Vietnamese Army soldiers attacked the southern outer walls on the 14th, but even with US air support, were repelled. On the 15th, foul weather weakened US air support, while Viet Cong reinforcements arrived through the unguarded western entrances to the city. By the 20th, casualties brought American forces to half strength. However, the Americans received good news during this period. On February 16, the ARVN/USAF intercepted an enemy radio signal and learned that the North Vietnamese leader inside the Citadel had been killed, and that the new commander wanted to withdraw. The new commander was refused permission to do so, but obviously, NVA/VC morale was depreciating.

February 21 brought better weather and the return of American air cover. United States soldiers in the area of Hue, but not in the city proper, pushed toward the Citadel and attacked from without. US and ARVN troops inside meanwhile pushed harder and by the 22nd reached the southern ramparts and the bridge over the Perfume River. Only the Imperial Palace remained in NVA/VC hands, and ARVN chose to finish the battle itself. After midnight on February 24, South Vietnamese Army forces successfully launched a surprise attack. An ARVN regiment replaced the Viet Cong flag in the Citadel with its own, and discovered early on the 25th that all NVA/VC troops had withdrawn. All that remained was to clean up scattered hold-outs in the Gia Hoi suburb to the east of the Citadel. The Battle for Hue officially ended.

Some correspondents traveling with the soldiers called the fighting in Hue the most intense in South Vietnam. Soldiers had little sleep, and the casualty rate was approximated at one casualty per yard of ground gained. Estimates of numbers of casualties varied with the sources. The Americans claimed 119 American, 363 South Vietnamese and 4,173 Viet Cong dead; ARVN/USAF wounded, they said, totalled 961 Americans and 1,242 South Vietnamese. At the same time, the North Vietnamese News Agency claimed more than 12,000 ARVN/USAF casualties.

Hue itself was devastated. Official estimates claim that close to 80 percent of the buildings in Hue were damaged. The

Machine gunner looks for snipers in (sic) the streets of southern Hue on the second day of the siege.

largely-ruined city left more than 100,000 people—over two-thirds of the city's population—homeless. Food supplies were depleted by February 25, forcing ARVN to transport emergency goods. And by some estimates, almost 6,000 civilians were killed or missing. Many were caught by ground crossfire and artillery or by American air bombings. Others, some of whose names had been gathered by NVA/VC intelligence prior to the attack, were killed by the Viet Cong for sympathizing with the other side.

During the time that the Viet Cong controlled the city, they appropriated all private radios in order to cut off communication, and they spread the rumor that all of Thua Thien Province had been completely captured. Simultaneously, the Viet Cong gathered citizens together, supposedly to re-indoctrinate them. Those people on the intelligence lists were pursued immediately; others were ordered to the so-called "political study meetings." These orders were issued with increasing urgency, until the NVA/VC threatened to kill those who were hiding.

Everyone at the meetings was divided into groups; citizens, police, soldiers, or civil servants. In the mildest instances, "citizens" were sent home while everyone else was kept overnight at the Government Delegates' office building. Much more serious proceedings took place in Gia Hoi. The North Vietnamese 1st Division had decided to let Gia Hoi wait until the Citadel had been retaken; however, the less intense fighting did not divert Viet Cong attention from political activities. In Gia Hoi, people were divided into the same categories as the rest of Hue. "Citizens" were told to form community groups, each with an enemy contact, in order to help control the people. The other groups were told to turn in all weapons and report to NVA/VC military police. Those who did so were allowed to return home. Two days later, however,

these former government employees were required to attend additional political meetings. Many disappeared completely.

According to a South Vietnamese report, more than 1,000 corpses were discovered in shallow mass graves scattered throughout the city, especially in the Bai Dau area and near Emperor Tu Doc's tomb. Other reports estimate the number of people killed at closer to 3,000, even 5,700. The victims, many of whom were tied together, had been shot, decapitated or buried alive. The corpses were identified as Vietnamese soldiers and civilians of various levels, and as foreigners, including Americans, mostly clergy and diplomatic personnel. Survivors and captured NVA/VC agents later explained that the meetings consisted of digging "air raid trenches," into which the prisoners were buried at nightfall.

These mass murders were denied by some Communist officials, who claimed that the corpses were the bodies of Viet Cong killed by South Vietnamese soldiers. Truong Nhu Tang, an NLF member now in exile in Paris, admitted the massacre occurred but claimed only that discipline had been lax and that the atrocities had not been ordered by the NLF. Tang later complained bitterly of having been betrayed by the Communists.

Some Americans implied that the number of deaths may have been exaggerated from the start. They noted that the majority of corpses were found by a South Vietnamese unit whose duty was to make the NLF look as bad as possible, and that more objective onlookers, such as reporters, were not allowed to see the mass graves. The American and South Vietnamese governments still insist that the Communists were responsible. In November 1969, President Nixon said that the "atrocities at Hue" were only "a prelude of what would happen in South Vietnam" should the Communists gain full control.

Wounded soldier is lowered down from his rooftop position in Hue.

Tanks roll into Hue as Vietnamese civilians flee.

Inside a house in Hue soldiers set up anti-sniper position with a 106mm recoiless rifle. Outside, infantrymen take whatever cover the city streets provide.

At left: Mortar team sends a 3.5 rocket round up
for launch from a rooftop.

Infantrymen with M-16s take aim at snipers in the streets of Hue.

At left: **Mobile mortar jeep fires into building in fighting that was door-to-door throughout the battle.** Below: **Soldiers take cover along wall surrounding private residence and garden in Hue.** At right: **Army driver signals left-hand turn.**

Sniper action ricochets in the streets of Hue.

At right: Soldier carries civilian casualty to army hospital during fighting in Hue. Opposite page: Wounded radio man gazes into the streets of Hue. Machine gunner stands behind him. Below: Patrol takes cover behind jeep during first week of fighting in Hue.

In order to provide ground support for infantry movement, the Marines used artillery fire and air strikes on the city of Hue. The NVA/VC quickly converted the rubble to ground cover. The resulting street battles were fierce as the Marines returned sniper fire with sniper fire. At left and opposite right, below: Machine gunners return sniper fire. Below: Cameraman catches the action on the streets as patrol takes cover. Opposite: Soldiers carry wounded man to safe cover.

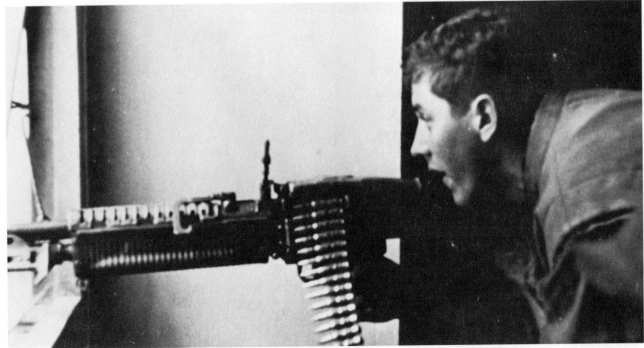

American casualties were heavy in the first few days of the siege of Hue, south of the Citadel, as Marines tried to isolate the NVA/VC defenders of the Citadel. Far left, top: Medic treats wounded soldier. Far left, below: Patrol takes cover in a hurry in south section of Hue. At left: Infantryman carrying mortar gun looks for position in the rubble. Below: Americans with flak vests fire their M-16s from cover of house.

By February 10, US troops had pushed the NVA/VC out of the new city in the south and into the Citadel. Except for sporadic sniper fire, the US troops concentrated on setting up long-range mortar positions to begin a siege to regain the Citadel. Below: Troops move mortar into position. Right: Infantryman moves into position around mortar base. Left, top and bottom: Troops hide behind available cover, such as trees and churches, in the last days of street fighting in the south city.

Block-to-block fighting continues in some sections of the south city as tanks roll in to begin
the assault on the Citadel across the river. Bullet
holes in the brick wall by the tank are an
indication of the level of sniper action around
the city.

Marines first crossed the Perfume River on February 11 and entered the northwest corner of the Citadel, while aircraft diverted enemy fire. Right: Marines cross the river in assault boat. Below: Tank units continue advance through the south city. Writing surrounding the tank designation reads "The original flower children."

The city of Hue was the ancestral capital of the Vietnamese. The Old City contained many buildings with ornate carvings. Below: US soldier fires his machine gun from behind a rooftop facade.

The NVA and the VC were entrenched in the Citadel. Machine gun fire was constantly brought to bear on the walls. Above: Troops relax in front of bullet-riddled building.

Intensive machine gun fighting continued for several days after the Marines crossed the river into the northern city and the Citadel. By the 15th of February, bad weather had made air support impossible and the Viet Cong had received reinforcements. American casualties were heavy for the next five days. Below: Machine gunners fire from behind a tree. Right: Everyone carries machine gun ammunition. Far right, above: Machine gun position is protected with bricks and sandbags. Far right, below: Tanks' forward progress is halted by destroyed bridge over one of the many canals.

By February 20th good weather returned and American soldiers pushed toward the Citadel. Above: American troops engage in sniper action using the M-16. Below: Mortar fire was used against the walls while tanks held back—providing nap time for tank crews.

Most troops marched into the Old City; some took more leisurely transportation.

Initially, American commanders banned air and mortar attacks on the Citadel, but they soon realized both were necessary.

Opposite left: **American soldier sits on the throne inside the Palace.** Opposite, below: **Church in Old City shows the effects of air strikes.** This page: **By February 29th, the Imperial Palace was taken and the battle for Hue was over. All that remained was to clean up scattered hold-outs in the Gia Hoi suburb east of the Citadel.**

Rockets are fired from the Tan Son Nhut air base during the Tet attack.

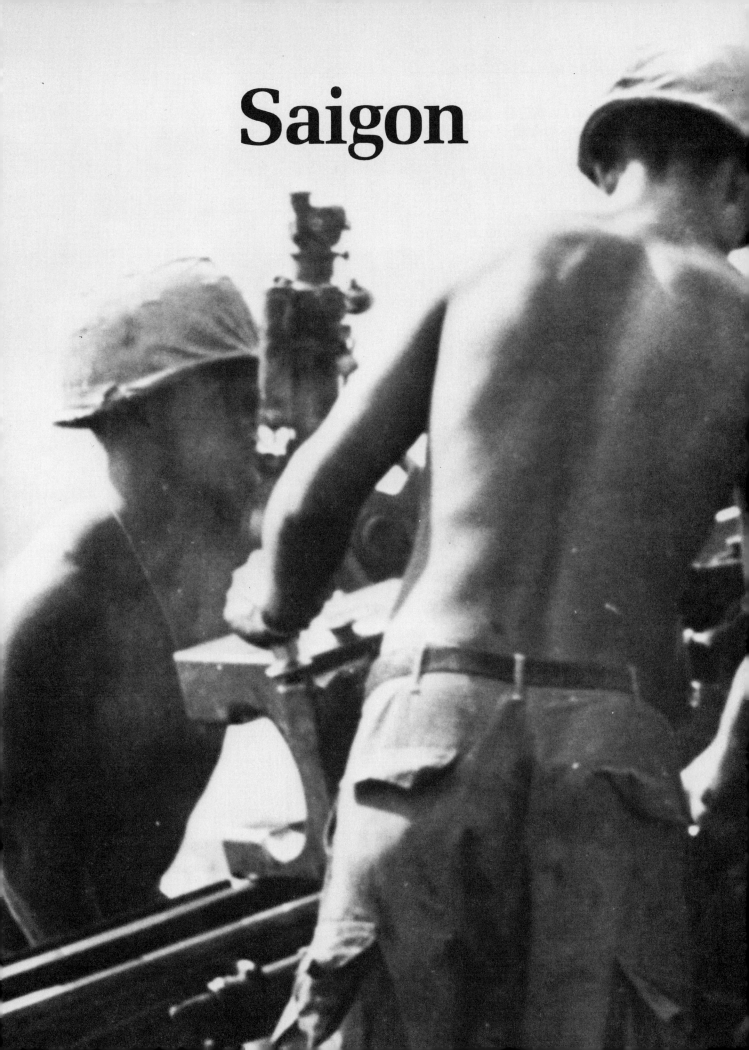

Saigon

By the end of 1967, Saigon was a booming city. Its economy had been bolstered by the war and by American aid and patronage. It was the seat of control and wealth in South Vietnam, although it was also marked by poverty and slums. Its population, at that time two million in the city and another one million in the surrounding suburbs, constituted one-fifth of the entire country's population and had been increasing for years due to its relative safety. The countryside bore the brunt of wartime destruction, and people fled to the protection of the city. In twenty years of civil war, except for rare instances of terrorism, the city had not been under fire.

Saigon was protected by ten ARVN battalions and 17 thousand National Police officers; it was surrounded by major American command centers, air fields, and bases. Its inhabitants, lulled into a feeling of security, were not especially worried about their safety after attacks on other cities on January 30, the eve of Tet, and they did not interrupt their new year's celebrating.

On December 15, 1967, the US had turned over the defense of Saigon to the South Vietnamese as a sign of confidence, an arrangement that benefitted both parties. The South Vietnamese did not want Americans defending the city because, in the event of a coup, they would have very little power or control, and the Americans wanted their troops free for planned offensive action against base camps near the Cambodian border in early 1968.

At the approach of Tet, approximately four to five thousand Viet Cong soldiers from local forces, who were familiar with Saigon and its people, had entered the city disguised as civilians joining their families for the holiday. Weapons and other supplies were smuggled into Saigon on trucks containing laundry or rice and tomatoes, and even hidden in coffins at fake funerals for South Vietnamese soldiers. Weapons tested in preparation for the attack during firework displays of the Tet celebration were not detected. South Vietnamese security was lax and the Viet Cong had no problem sneaking in with supplies and keeping them hidden.

The American command had become suspicious that the enemy was planning something against Saigon. Early in January, probes by US forces around Viet Cong bases near the Cambodian border did not meet with as much resistance as they usually did. Also, enemy radio transmissions were picked up close to Saigon. Lieutenant General Frederick C. Weyand, commander of US field forces in III Corps, was concerned by this unusual activity and convinced General Westmoreland to move troops that had been assigned to border regions closer to Saigon. Weyand had never agreed with the strategy of massing troops at the border, and Westmoreland also had begun to doubt its necessity due to intelligence findings, so did not hesitate to redeploy some troops. Westmoreland later called this one of the most critical strategies of the war.

On Tuesday, January 30, at 9:15 PM, South Vietnamese troops captured a Viet Cong soldier carrying three Soviet Ak-47 rifles just outside Saigon. He admitted that the Tan Son Nhut air base and the government radio station were going to be attacked. Weyand notified US division commanders to be on alert.

Because of Weyand's order, five marines, instead of the usual four, were guarding the American Embassy in Saigon on January 31. The embassy had been rebuilt in 1965 after a bombing and was supposed to be impenetrable. It was surrounded by an eight foot wall and encased in concrete rocket shield and shatterproof Plexiglass windows. Despite these fortifications, nineteen Viet Cong infiltrators from the C-10 Sapper Battalion forced their way into the compound in what has become the most well-known assault of the Battle of Saigon. Sappers, i.e., specialists in penetrating for-

tifications, blasted a rocket through the embassy wall and entered the compound at 2:30 AM, immediately killing the two MPs standing guard at the gate. Within a few minutes, three more American Marines were killed. But the Viet Cong got no farther. The leaders of the unit were killed in the initial confrontation and once the sappers made their way into the compound they became disorganized. Viet Cong never got into the chancery building. Marines defended the embassy until a detachment of the 101st Airborne Division landed on the roof of the chancery to secure it.

Allen Wendt, the ranking American diplomat in the embassy that night, was a junior economics specialist doing routine night work at the time of the attack. He locked himself in a fortified code room until the fighting was over. American Ambassador Ellsworth Bunker was not at the embassy when it was attacked, and was moved from his house to a subordinate's house for safety. Colonel George Jacobson, without a weapon, was on the second floor of a villa behind the chancery building. He was thrown a gun to use against a Viet Cong soldier, who was seen approaching him on a flight of outside stairs. Jacobson shot the man who turned out to be the last Viet Cong rebel still on the loose in the embassy compound.

The Americans did not want to take any chances that more Viet Cong remained in the vicinity, so Marines were ordered to kill anyone in the compound who was not American. All 19 Viet Cong rebels were killed or captured, as were two South Vietnamese chauffeurs who were unfortunate to be in the compound after this order was issued. Later, the defense of the embassy was referred to as the "Battle for Bunker's Bunker."

Viet Cong and North Vietnamese forces launched their heaviest attack in the Saigon area against the Tan Son Nhut air base. This air base, which was north of the city, was headquarters for the Military Assistance Command Vietnam and the 7th Air Force. It was adjacent to South Vietnam's Joint General Staff (JGS) headquarters which is equivalent to the American Joint Chiefs of Staff.

The surprise attack came from the north, east, and west and started around 3 AM. North Vietnamese and Viet Cong troops came within 1000 yards of the 7th Air Force headquarters before being challenged. Two companies of the ARVN 8th Airborne Battalion were waiting at the air base to fly north to help South Vietnamese forces there; however, their flight had been delayed so they were quickly in place to defend the base. The fighting was so intense that Westmoreland's staff joined in, and he was moved to a windowless command bunker. So great was the surprise of the attack that eighty percent of the soldiers at Tan Son Nhut, including the general's staff, had to go to the supply room to get weapons and ammunition before they could begin to defend the base. The ARVN airborne and American security forces remained in control of the air base, although they suffered heavy casualties.

North Vietnamese soldiers made their way to the gate of the Joint General Staff compound disguised as ARVN soldiers. The real South Vietnamese soldiers barricaded themselves in until help arrived; most who were killed there were shot by weapons they had set up to guard the headquarters and which were turned on them by the North Vietnamese.

It was very important for South Vietnam that the North Vietnamese not take over the compound because President Thieu, Vice-President Ky, and most high ranking military and cabinet ministers were gathered there. Viet Cong agents had orders to assassinate Thieu, Ambassador Ellsworth Bunker, chief of South Vietnamese Central Intelligence General Linh Quang Vien, chief of National Police Brigadier General Nguyen Ngoc Loan, and chief of Saigon Police Lieutenant Colonel Nguyen Van Luan. All assassination attempts failed— one squad got lost and another became separated from its weapons—but three rockets penetrated the compound and came close to killing most of South Vietnam's leadership.

After South Vietnamese soldiers from the Mekong Delta and an American armored squadron from the 25th Infantry Division arrived as reinforcements, the combination of dive bombers, armed helicopters, tanks, and ground troops forced the NVA/VC to retreat to a Vinatexco cotton mill. The mill was soon destroyed and 162 bodies were found in the ruins.

The most organized NVA/VC assault was against the national radio station. Dang Xuan Teo, a member of the Viet Cong group that attacked the station, later said that they had planned for 15 to 20 Viet Cong sappers and an experienced NVA radioman to take over the station and play tapes announcing that Saigon had been liberated and the general uprising had begun. They were expected to hold the station for approximately two hours until support arrived. An employee of the radio station had given keys and a detailed layout of the building to the Viet Cong. Government soldiers positioned on the roof to protect the station were gunned down by Viet Cong soldiers from an apartment building overlooking the station. The insurgents entered the building dressed as South Vietnamese riot police. As soon as one of the technicians realized what was happening, he notified station personnel at a transmitter 14 miles away to cut off the studio's broadcasts. A prearranged signal had been devised the previous afternoon by Lieutenant Colonel Vu Duc Vinh, director-general of the radio station, for such an emergency.

The Viet Cong got into the main control room, where the United States had recently installed $1 million worth of equipment. Quickly realizing that they could not broadcast their message, they began to destroy the system. Teo, in recounting the episode, said that after the supply of ammunition was depleted and he was sure reinforcements would not arrive, he escaped to search for help. Before he returned, South Vietnamese paratroopers set the station on fire, and killed the infiltrators as they tried to escape. The South Vietnamese soldiers then looted whatever equipment was left after they gained control.

Vinh exhibited foresight in his plan for

shutting down the radio station in case of attack, but neither he nor anyone else made arrangements for broadcasts of information from the transmission site as a substitute for the usual radio program. Consequently, while Hanoi Radio and Liberation (Viet Cong) Radio were transmitting reports of widespread attacks and pleas for people to join the uprising, Saigon Radio was playing anything personnel at the transmission site could find: Viennese waltzes, Beatles and Rolling Stones songs, and Vietnamese martial music.

While the embassy, radio station, and Tan Son Nhut air base were the scenes of the heaviest fighting, other locations in Saigon were also under fire. The presidential palace was attacked by thirteen men and one woman. After being quickly forced back from the gate, they barricaded themselves in a partially completed apartment building across the street from the palace for more than fifteen hours. By the end of the siege, most of the rebels were dead.

This assault played well on the news. It was a rare instance when journalists were in a position to film a siege in progress, especially in daylight. All three American networks carried clips on it. In order to get the footage, they had to buy time on a commercial communications satellite and then have it relayed from Tokyo where an Air Force medical evacuation plane had flown the film. The minimum cost for access to the palace footage was $4,031. An American official calculated after the Tet Offensive was over that the Viet Cong had spent $3,980 on all of the weapons, ammunition, and explosives used by them against the palace—$51 less for the entire assault than American newscasts spent for a few minutes of film.

Hole shows where Viet Cong sappers blasted through the embassy wall and entered the compound.

Bodies of Viet Cong infiltrators lie on embassy grounds.

There were other less significant Viet Cong assaults throughout the city. For example, a battalion of Viet Cong were supposed to take over the Saigon prison and free its 5,000 prisoners, many who were there on political charges. On the way to the prison the "liberators" encountered enemy troops and never made it there. Also, two battalions of Viet Cong took control of the South Vietnamese Armored Command headquarters and the Artillery Command headquarters with the idea of using the tanks and howitzers there against the Tan Son Nhut air base and other targets. When they entered the Armored Command headquarters, they discovered that the tanks had been moved a few months earlier, and in the Artillery Command headquarters, soldiers had removed breechblocks from the howitzers to make them unusable before abandoning them.

The headquarters of the South Vietnamese Navy was likewise attacked with similar results. A Viet Cong survivor recounted that reinforcements had been expected, this time from across the Saigon River. Not only did they not arrive, but there was never even a trace of a battalion in the area from which they were supposed to originate. Long Binh Post, the location of Weyand's headquarters, and the Tactical Operation Center was fired upon early in the siege but NVA/VC forces were again repulsed.

City people whose homes were destroyed gravitated towards the center of Saigon. Police were forced to put up barricades to prevent dangerous overcrowding. President Thieu declared martial law and established a curfew in Saigon and nearby Cholon. In some sections of the city, NVA/VC soldiers searched houses for government officials or Americans hidden by civilians. Often, American soldiers were in close pursuit. ARVN/USAF soldiers who were captured by the North Vietnamese/Viet Cong were tried, sentenced and executed in front of civilians, to demonstrate what happened to enemies of the Vietnamese people. Conversely, some Viet Cong prisoners were shot immediately after being captured as a warning against helping the NLF.

A well known photograph by Eddie Adams, an AP photographer, and film footage by Vo Suu, a Vietnamese cameraman working for NBC, shocked American viewers when they saw the chief of South Vietnam's National Police, Nguyen Ngoc Loan, execute a Viet Cong prisoner. The film showed a group of government troops walking a Viet Cong prisoner toward Loan, who waved bystanders away and without hesitation shot the prisoner in the head. It later became known that the prisoner was a Viet Cong officer and that Loan had lost several National Police, including one whose family had been killed with him in their home. Pictures of the scene were in papers throughout the United States, and NBC showed the edited film clip during its regular evening broadcast, adding some editorial touches of its own such as the sound of a gunshot. Most viewers were appalled at what seemed to be a brutal act carried out by one of America's allies. The US embassy stopped such executions out of fear that the NVA/VC would do the same to American prisoners.

Between February 3 and 5, the atmosphere in Saigon began to relax. The curfew was partially lifted and, except for American support personnel and MPs, control of Saigon was returned to the South Vietnamese, while US forces concentrated on surrounding areas. The largest mass of NVA/VC troops left was in the Chinese suburb of Cholon, where a large Buddhist population had long been in opposition to the South Vietnamese government. The government suspected that this area was the base from which the attack on Saigon originated, and they recommended that Cholon be destroyed. On February 13, with NVA/VC forces still controlling Cholon, American B-52s bombed it. The raid killed 42 people, but MACV admitted that they were not sure whether or not they were civilians. On February 18, the NVA/VC forces staged a counteroffensive in Cholon and again unsuccessfully attacked Tan Son Nhut air base. But by February 23, ARVN/USAF forces had driven out all opposing troops who had entered Saigon and Cholon during Tet.

Transportation around the country, as well as civilian life within the cities, was affected by the Tet Offensive. Highways were closed by roadblocks and sabotage. Convoys, stopped at outlying posts, were detained for over two days as they waited for engineers to clear or repair the roads. Vietnamese drivers, afraid of reprisals, refused to work, bringing trucking to a halt, even where roads were passable. River barges normally serving the delta region were held up and railway movement across the country came to a complete standstill. Aircraft provided the only reliable transportation throughout the region; routine requests were pushed aside while emergency and combat movement took precedence.

MPs swarm the embassy after the attack. Only five Marines were on guard around the compound at the time of the attack.

During the attack on the embassy, five Marines were killed, as were two South Vietnamese chauffeurs. By morning all Viet Cong infiltrators were dead (above) or had been taken prisoners.

Left: The front entrance of the embassy shows effect of enemy fire and destruction of the shield of the US. Below: Fighting around BOQ #3 on the outskirts of Saigon continues.

Remains of Viet Cong infiltrator lies in embassy rubble.

Embassy staff member surveys damage to the entrance. The dead Viet Cong remain for the press reporters and photographers. Officials hoped that the widespread press coverage would play well in the States. In fact, the opposite reaction occurred.

Security at the embassy for several days following the attack was very heavy.

As US troops moved into the city, Vietnamese fled their homes.

The Viet Cong launched their heaviest attack against the Tan Son Nhut air base north of Saigon at 3 AM January 31. Airmen of the 7th Air Force (above and right) defended the base until armored reinforcements arrived (below).

Troops move the defensive perimeter out and encounter dead Viet Cong guerrillas. A body count was a grim task but the results were anxiously awaited and widely reported by the press.

Above: An armored squadron of the 25th Infantry Division arrived with tanks, helicopters and bombers, as well as troops to help in the defense. Viet Cong guerrillas lie in the road in the foreground.

Left: South Vietnamese soldiers arrived shortly after the attack on the air base to help in the defense.

Many sections of downtown Saigon were also
under fire from Viet Cong attack, however
within a few days the siege ended in most sections of the city. Left: Casualties await transportation in a suburb of Saigon. Below: Tanks
patrol the streets of downtown Saigon.

Troops patrol a cemetery looking for snipers on the day after the initial attack.

Armored personnel carriers from the 25th Infantry Division enter the city of Saigon on February 1. Inset: Soldier returns sniper fire with M-14 at Long Binh post.

At Tan Son Nhut air base both American and
NVA/VC casualties are heavy.

More than 700 NVA/VC troops attacked Tan Son Nhut. Although they took the 7th Air Force completely by surprise, the defenders repulsed the attack quickly. Most of the infiltrators were killed in the assault. Inset: APC and troops move in to protect Long Binh, the command post for General Weyland, commander of III Corps.

Aerial view of the Saigon suburb of Cholon shows effects of air strikes near the soccer stadium in early February 1968.

A closer view of Cholon shows that the destruction was devastating to the residences. Homes were obliterated and only a few buildings stood after a direct hit. Inset: M-14 is used in the defense of Long Binh post.

Armored squadron regiment moves out to take up positions around the Phu Thu Race Track in a "Duster" tank refitted with 40mm cannon.

Company commander assigns positions to platoon leaders in early morning briefing.

A platoon from the 7th Infantry Regiment patrols the streets in Cholon in early February.

UH 1-Bs, or Hueys, take off from the Phi Thu Race Track outside Saigon. Inset: Vietnamese children examine the rubble of what was once their homes.

Although the casualties were heavy on the perimeter, damage to the Tan Son Nhut air base itself was not extensive. Some enemy rocket fire, however, did disrupt the runway and destroy some planes.

Airman inspects rocket damage to airfield. A Camberra jet sits undamaged in the background.

Close-up shows exploded rocket shell on runway at Tan Son Nhut.

A C-47 suffered a direct hit from rocket fire at Tan Son Nhut air base while transport plane next to it was undamaged. Insets: Mortar attacks did destroy some planes.

Other Cities

Troops enjoy a break atop their APCs outside Da Nang.

Hue and Saigon were the two most important cities attacked during Tet; however, they were by no means the only cities attacked. Although exact figures vary with the sources, an estimated 100 to 110 cities were attacked on the 30th and 31st of January.

Two hours after the Tet truce was cancelled, Da Nang was attacked by rocket fire. Sections of the suburbs were destroyed in house-to-house fighting, and a bombing raid damaged I Corps headquarters but left the building intact. In another raid the next day against the corps headquarters, the NVA/VC went further into the Da Nang complex than they had gone in three years. This attack destroyed five aircraft; eighteen more were destroyed in a later rocket attack on the airstrip. The NVA/VC were driven out of the city on the 31st of January. Like the city of Hue, Da Nang had been part of the 1966 Buddhist revolt; therefore, over 200 people were detained by the ARVN/USAF for helping the VC.

Another small city attacked was Nha Trang, hit first by a mortar barrage and, much later in the night, entered by 800 soldiers of the North Vietnamese Army. Infiltrators captured the province administration headquarters. In an attempt to regain the building, ARVN/USAF troops set it afire. Twenty-eight hours after the initial attack, the city was cleared of the attack force.

Attacks along the coast included the seaside towns of Hoi An and Qui Nhon, previously perceived as beyond the reach of the NVA/VC. Though fighting lasted less than two days, Hoi An was attacked by two battalions of the NLF main force.

In the central coastal region, Qui Nhon, Tuy Hoa, and Nha Trang all were temporarily occupied by the invaders, who destroyed buildings and released hundreds of political prisoners. Airlift operations to fields in the area, such as Nha Trang, were halted only briefly, but did experience delays at other times. Even when fighting was close enough for air crews to watch it as they landed and tookoff, airlifts continued.

The NVA/VC attacked Kontum, Pleiku and Ban Me Thuot, occupying the cities briefly but giving up after only a few days' fight. Fighting the first day at Kontum and Ban Me Thuot was very heavy. Late into the afternoon of the 31st, an emergency airlift supplied and reinforced the Ban Me Thuot defenders. Attackers held both the military and civilian airfields, and encircled the local military headquarters. Despite inclement weather, troops of the 23d Ranger Battalion were transported from Bao Loc, also under fire, to Ban Me Thuot by dawn of February 1 in an unprecedented emergency night troop movement under small arms and mortar fire.

The resupply situation in Kontum was equally difficult, when the city was dangerously short of ammunition by the 2nd, a drop zone was established where, under fire and covered by darkness, aircrews were able to bring in over five tons of munitions.

Road travel to Pleiku and Dak To was halted as traffic was harassed by sabotage, land mines, and frequent ambushes. Fighting ended at Kontum on the 4th, at Ban Me Thuot on the 6th, and at Dalat on the 10th. By the 11th of February, road activity in the region had returned to normal.

The NVA/VC's second offensive began on February 18. Forty-seven towns and military installations were attacked during this assault which was limited to mortar and artillery bombardments, and some use of infantry. Only Binh Thuan Province, where the VC released over 500 political prisoners, was overrun by the attackers; however, they were forced back two days later.

Troops wade through typical terrain outside Da Nang looking for Viet Cong. The entrenching tool, close-at-hand in the packs, was often a soldier's best friend.

Troops land in Da Nang aboard
an APC ready for action. Inset:
Airman examines damage
done to revetment by 122mm
rocket fire during Tet attack in
Da Nang.

Perhaps as many as 110 individual cities were attacked on the night of January 31 as part of the Tet Offensive. Two hours after the Tet truce was cancelled, Da Nang (bottom right) was attacked by rocket fire. Pleiku was attacked and briefly occupied for a few days, during which significant damage was done to the 71st Evacuation Hospital (below and right).

Artillery unit returns fire from the Carroll camp near Khe Sanh.

Khe Sanh

Increased enemy activity was detected in the Khe Sanh area near the DMZ in December and early January, prior to a major attack in the middle of the month before the Tet holidays. Several theories explain General Giap's motives for attacking Khe Sanh at the time and manner in which he did. Perhaps he realized the similarities between Khe Sanh and Dien Bien Phu and wanted to undermine the Americans as he had the French. Perhaps he appreciated the location of the base and wanted to use it as a jumping off point from which to take over Quang Tri and Thua Thien provinces and the rest of South Vietnam.

In early January as Westmoreland and Bunker prepared for the 36-hour Tet truce, they took care to exclude I Corps from those plans, in large part because they anticipated a siege attempt at Khe Sanh, a Marine base located in Quang Tri Province approximately 14 miles from the DMZ and six miles from the Laos border. The terrain around the base was mountainous, with lush forests and tall elephant grass immediately surrounding the base. About 3,500 men were stationed at the base under the command of Marine Corps Colonel David E. Lownds. They controlled several hills surrounding the base.

ARVN/USAF learned a few weeks before the attack on Khe Sanh that the NVA/VC were planning something big. Marines at a small outpost of the Khe Sanh found six unfamiliar soldiers wandering around the camp on January 2. The strangers, later identified as North Vietnamese officers, were dressed as American Marines but refused to answer the sentries' English questions. When one stranger appeared to be grabbing a grenade, the Marines from the camp shot him and his companions. Five died; one escaped. Word was sent to MACV immediately that NVA officers were personally patrolling territory.

Within two more days, reports arrived that new NVA regiments were moving into the mountains around Khe Sanh. Several more regiments moved into the area by the end of the month, including the 304th Division, an elite unit which had served during

Dien Bien Phu thirteen years earlier. The Marines at the base established during this period of preparation a routine that lasted them for most of the siege. Their days consisted of short patrols and of reinforcing the bunkers and trenches.

On January 5, Westmoreland ordered the development of a massive aerial bombardment program. The operation was entitled NIAGARA "to evoke an image of cascading bombs and shells" and would be carried out in two parts. The first part, Niagara I, was a comprehensive intelligence effort to find enemy locations in northern I Corps and the area immediately west of the Laotian border. All available sources were utilized,

Although the defense of Khe Sanh has just begun, some Marines appear to be getting ready to leave aboard an Air Force C-130 Hercules in early February 1968.

such as interrogation of prisoners and anybody else that was in or passed through the area, the study of captured enemy documents, and high-resolution photographs. Information also was obtained with the help of the United States Navy, Marines, and Air Force reconnaissance, using tactical and electronically equipped aircraft. The methods of searching for targets was so extensive that they included acoustic sensors to pick up voices; seismic sensors to determine vibrations from marching soldiers, trucks, and tanks; infrared heat sensors to find cooking fires; and electrochemical analyzers to detect high concentrations of human urine. Technicians in an airborne laboratory

compiled the data and passed it on to MACV headquarters in Saigon. The information collected in Niagara I produced an average of 150 recommended targets daily.

On January 20, a defector from the NVA told Khe Sanh commanders that the base was to be a second Dien Bien Phu. First Lieutenant La Than Tonc said that the attack was to start that same night. He described in detail the plans for several NVA regiments . . . and he was right. Tonc also said that the main assault on the base would come at Tet. (In fact, Khe Sanh was about the only place in South Vietnam that was not heavily attacked at Tet.)

The allusion to Dien Bien Phu was an appropriate means of encouraging Americans to deploy extra troops and resources at Khe Sanh. Many feared that the Communists were planning to gain a psychological victory over the American people by winning a military victory at the base and consequently breaking down American support for the war. Westmoreland's decision to put up a big defensive at Khe Sanh resulted from fear of a repeat of the French debacle.

The siege of Khe Sanh began at 5:30 AM on January 21, eight days before the NVA/VC launched the main thrust of the Tet Offensive. On this day, Westmoreland decided to implement Niagara II, the second phase of the Niagara operation, which initiated a deluge of bombing attacks. It constituted the greatest amount of aerial bombing ever dropped on one tactical location. Its execution required 2,000 strategic and tactical aircraft as diverse as B-52s and prop-driven South Vietnamese A-1 Skyraiders, as well as 3,000 helicopters. The raids were organized by "Sky Spot," an airborne computer control center that was capable of directing the altitudes and speeds of 800 aircraft at a time. Westmoreland selected the targets himself. According to the US command, the B-52 raids were vital to the success of Niagara II. The bombings resulted in high casualty rates and created fear and low morale among enemy troops while raising confidence among American units. The Army believed that the raids forced large numbers of NVA/VC troops to evacuate

positions which had involved a great deal of time and resources to prepare.

The defense of Khe Sanh depended on Niagara II and the ability to bring in supplies. Supplies were a problem because overland routes to the base had been cut off since August of the previous year; airlift was the primary means of transport to and from Khe Sanh. Troops increased efforts to reopen Route 9 in case weather prohibited airlifted provisions, although they did not succeed in reopening the road until early April.

The NVA/VC attacked the Khe Sanh base with a variety of heavy weapons and quickly destroyed most of the base's supply of ammunition and much of its fuel. Several helicopters were ruined or damaged, and there were almost 60 American casualties. The airstrip was damaged, and the enemy continued to fire anti-aircraft guns. Both sides rushed in reinforcements and supplies. Within days, Khe Sanh housed more than 5,000 American soldiers and tons of supplies and ammunition. When January ended, approximately 6,000 men were in Khe Sanh. Enemy forces surrounding the base were estimated at 20,000 to 50,000 regular-army North Vietnamese soldiers.

Despite intense debate at all levels about the worth of the base, Westmoreland and Lieutenant General Robert E. Cushman, Jr., Commander of III Marine Amphibious Force, decided to defend Khe Sanh. A battle at Khe Sanh was an economical way to kill large numbers of North Vietnamese—they assumed only one reinforced Marine regiment would be necessary to do the job. A battle at Khe Sanh was also attractive because set battles seemed to be the only kind in which Americans could win. An American victory at Khe Sanh was also important for keeping the NVA/VC from taking over the provinces closest to North Vietnam, Quang Tri and Thua Thien. Westmoreland explained his decision to defend the base:

The question was whether we could afford the troops to reinforce, keep them supplied by air, and defeat an enemy far superior in numbers as we waited for the weather to clear, built forward bases, and made other preparations for an overland relief expedition. I believed we could do all these things. With concurrence of the III Marine Amphibious Commander Lieutenant General Robert E. Cushman, Jr., I made the decision to reinforce and hold the area while destroying the enemy with our massive firepower and to prepare for offensive operations when the weather became favorable.

Once this decision was made, President Johnson haunted Westmoreland and General Wheeler in search of assurance that Khe Sanh would not turn into another Dien Bien Phu. Johnson's repeated questions about supplies and reinforcements led Westmoreland to make daily, detailed reports regarding the status of the Marine base. Ironically, the Marines at the base favored withdrawal. They felt their job was to keep under surveillance the Ho Chi Minh Trail across the border in Laos; under siege, they could not accomplish that aim.

On January 22, the NVA/VC aimed mortar at the base and at Hill 881, one of the several American-controlled hills surrounding Khe Sanh. Attempts by the Americans to destroy the enemy's weapons resulted only in the destruction of ARVN/USAF air equipment. The NVA/VC attacked a Laotian unit in Laos on the same day, forcing the Laotian soldiers and their families to take refuge at the Special Forces camp at Lang Vei, about 9 kilometers from Khe Sanh. The soldiers helped the Green Berets to defend their camp, but the Americans refused to believe the newcomers that the North Vietnamese had tanks. At the same time, Marine units were moved to a post at Phu Bai which would later be very important to the defense of Hue.

Thick fog cover allowed the North Vietnamese/Viet Cong to begin on the 24th to sneak closer to the base until the air strip was only 1,000 feet away; they began to fire mortar at the strip, usually while vehicles were on the ground or landing. Soon base personnel knew when aircraft were approaching by the anti-aircraft fire outside.

ARVN/USAF commanders feared that the NVA/VC would use their new positions as bases for a final assault. All US air forces were then ordered to the Khe Sanh area, away from North Vietnam, to bomb the enemy before such an attack could take place. The elite ARVN Rangers came to the base to fill in gaps in the defense. Their orders were to fight to the death should Khe Sanh be captured.

Offensive activity throughout South Vietnam decreased as the new year and truce approached. At Khe Sanh, the NVA/VC continued to bombard the base, although no new attacks were launched during Tet itself. Increased radio communication from the other side of the Laotian border in late January led American and South Vietnamese intelligence to believe that NVA headquarters for the Khe Sanh attackers was nearby. Westmoreland ordered a bomb strike on January 30 to destroy the enemy base at the indicated coordinates.

There were no more radio transmissions from that area. Some officials wondered if a large Tet assault on Khe Sanh would have originated at the base in Laos if it had not been bombed. NVA officers captured later claimed that the Tet attacks on January 30 in

Marines discuss the situation at Khe Sanh in early February.

I Corps and II Corps occurred earlier than elsewhere because of the bombings at the base, which confused the North Vietnamese/Viet Cong command structure.

In February, three major battles took place in the surrounding hills. The first was a heavy hand-to-hand fight on February 5, when enemy troops entered the perimeter of Hill 861A.

The most serious ground attack was on the Special Forces camp at Lang Vei. The NVA/VC attacked just after midnight on the 7th with Soviet-made tanks. This was the first time the NVA/VC used armor. Among the weapons at Lang Vei were several anti-tank guns, but many defenders did not know how to use them, and some reports indicated that a few guns would not fire. The 24 Green Berets, 900 Montagnards and the Laotian refugee troops continued to defend the base with smaller weapons; Khe Sanh Marines were asked to help. Fighter planes were sent from Khe Sanh during daylight hours, but, afraid that the attack on Lang Vei was just a prelude to a larger attack throughout the area, no more relief was sent. The commander at the camp, Captain Frank Willoughby, told his men to escape as best they could. By late the next morning, the camp was empty. Fourteen Green Berets and 60 Montagnards made it to Khe Sanh safely.

The army reported that almost half of the forces at Lang Vei, originally about 500, were missing or dead but that at least the enemy suffered as much of a loss. Survivors from the village Lang Vei, including the Laotians and civilian refugees, went to Khe Sanh, where they were first refused entry, but from where they later were evacuated.

The third main ground assault against a mountain post took place early on February 8 against a Marine platoon. Although the defenders initially lost some ground at the perimeter, they kept control of most of their territory and regained the rest before noon. Even so, the commander back at Khe Sanh decided the mountain position was too open and withdrew the defenders.

Also on the 8th of February, a three-day attack was launched against Khe Sanh itself.

American bombers continued shelling the outskirts of the base, but the enemy moved closer, achieving some positions only 33 feet from the perimeter.

On the 10th, an aircraft bringing fresh supplies to the base was shot down. The plane and some people aboard were lost. Soon afterwards new systems of delivery were adopted which did not require the aircraft to complete a landing, thereby allowing deliveries over a damaged airstrip and giving enemy guns less of a target. In one system, GPES (Ground Proximity Extraction System), pilots flew low over runways as ropes attached to their loads were grabbed by a hook implanted in the ground, causing the cargo to tumble out. Another, more frequently used, method was called LAPES (Low Altitude Parachute Extraction System). When pallets of provisions were released from plane tailgates, small parachutes tripped reefed-cargo parachutes to yank loads from the planes. Air force pilots, flying most of these supply missions because of their greater experience than Marine pilots, learned by experience or by word of mouth where the heaviest NVA/VC guns were along the airstrip. Both LAPES and GPES required good visibility; therefore, most deliveries were made by simple parachute drops due to poor weather.

Late in February, a Marine patrol found a network of tunnels leading towards Khe Sanh. A thick fog had enveloped the base for several previous days, during which the NVA/VC kept provision-laden helicopters from landing while they dug. The United States command was sensitive to this tactic because it confirmed fears that Khe Sanh was going to be a reenactment of Dien Bien Phu, so they ordered heavy bombing in the areas where they believed the tunnels were located. When the weather cleared and the Americans had the chance to examine the work of the NVA/VC troops, they discovered that the tunnels had been deserted for weeks.

The commanders at Khe Sanh anticipated a large attack before the end of February. Improving weather and longer days facilitated air support, and they knew that enough enemy units were positioned around Khe Sanh for a substantial offensive. On the 29th, sensors revealed movement of NVA/VC troops in the area. That night North Vietnamese/Viet Cong troops attacked three times, but were repelled each time.

Following that last big ground attack, the enemy was quieter, limiting action to harassing the Marines. By mid-March, the enemy appeared to be withdrawing. When Westmoreland began offensive action, the NVA/VC regiments left in haste. A last major confrontation on March 30 was a successful attack by the ARVN/USAF on an enemy camp.

As the Tet emergency faded, MACV could plan more effectively for the relief of Khe Sanh. The strategy was named Pegasus, and April 1 was chosen as the target date to rescue the besieged base. Logistical support to facilitate the transfer of supplies during the operation was provided by a US Army Support Command base near Ca Lu. To insure continued supplies throughout the operation, the Ca Lu base was well stocked before Pegasus began.

Pegasus involved the US 1st Air Cavalry Division, the 1st Marine Regiment and South Vietnamese airborne troops. On March 8, 1968, Westmoreland appointed General William W. Momyer, US Air Force, as the single manager for control of tactical air resources in South Vietnam, including Marine aircraft. The Marine Corps was not pleased with Westmoreland's decision. The commanding general of the III Marine Amphibious Force argued that it was not a necessary assignment and that the position interfered with his ability to carry out his orders. Operation Pegasus went into effect on April 1.

The 1st Cavalry landed about 10 miles east of Khe Sanh, establishing headquarters there. Their mission included reopening Route 9 and doing a final cleanup of the area, as well as relieving Khe Sanh. At the same time, Route 547, an old road that ran from Hue to the A Shau Valley, was cut off while the valley was checked for possible

enemy targets for additional air strikes. NVA/VC bases were located along the road in late March, and an alternate route, 547A, which had been built by NVA/VC soldiers, was discovered running from the A Shau Valley towards Hue.

Unopposed US and ARVN troops made their way towards Khe Sanh, clearing mines and examining former NVA/VC posts, while companies of engineers followed repairing Route 9. Although Operation Niagara ended when Pegasus began, air support for the new plan continued. On the first day, eight B-52 raids were flown to assist the Marines, along with 66 fighter sorties for tactical support, and twelve Air Force cargo planes. Also, 24 helicopters delivered almost 150 tons of supplies despite inclement weather.

On April 4, the Marine 1st Battalion of the 5th Cavalry attacked an old French fort held by NVA/VC forces. The next day American forces were put on the defensive for the first time during Pegasus when a NVA division attacked Hill 471, a site which the Marines had just reached the previous afternoon. The Marines, with artillery and air support, had no trouble repulsing the enemy. Meanwhile, defenders of the old French fort were continuing their struggle, but on April 7, after the 2nd Battalion replaced the 1st, the NVA/VC finally were defeated and the last significant threat to the Khe Sanh was eliminated. On April 8, the relief of Khe Sanh was completed and Route 9 was cleared. The enemy withdrew, although not without a few minor struggles. Finally, on April 14, US Marines attacked NVA/VC forces at Hill 881 and prevailed. This, the final battle of Pegasus, ironically occurred in the same location where the battle for Khe Sanh began on January 20.

The battle for Khe Sanh lasted 77 days. It should be noted, however, that in the most technical sense, Khe Sanh was never under siege, for Marines were never prevented from patrolling the area within 500 meters outside the base's perimeter.

Westmoreland announced to the President in Washington on April 11 that Route 9 was reopened and the battle was over. On

April 15, Operation Pegasus officially ended. Throughout the fighting, Army and Marines soldiers fired 158,891 rounds of artillery, ten times as many as were fired at them. The Air Force flew 9,691 runs, the Marines 7,078, and the Navy 5,337. Yet, Westmoreland reiterated at the end of the siege that it was the massive attacks by the B-52s that crippled the enemy forces. Throughout the entire siege, more than 75,000 tons of explosives were dropped on NVA/VC positions.

In examining the Pegasus operation, the US Army concluded that five factors contributed to its success: First, it was well planned. Second, the enemy was slow to react to the air mobility of the Americans, which permitted large numbers of troops and artillery to be maneuvered around and behind enemy lines. Third, the massive bombing and air support complemented the ground forces. Fourth, movement of supplies to the base was never interrupted. Finally, the Army concluded, the individual soldier never lost his determination and courage.

On June 17, Marines began stripping the base. When the American press discovered this they demanded an explanation for the military's abandoning a supposedly important tactical position. The military responded that the enemy was following a different strategy that made an established base at Khe Sanh unnecessary.

On June 27, all US troops withdrew from Khe Sanh. The NVA/VC quickly reoccupied it.

Many comparisons were made between the battle at Dien Bien Phu in 1954 and the battle at Khe Sanh. General Westmoreland was convinced that the Communists were maneuvering to obtain a strong bargaining position in peace talks. He had military officials and staff study the history of Dien Bien Phu. However, after listening to a lecture that presented a bleak picture, Westmoreland ended discussion because he was adamant that history would not repeat itself; the US would not be defeated.

Johnson also worried about a repeat of Dien Bien Phu. He had been a member of the Senate Armed Services Committee in 1954 and had opposed US intervention on behalf of the French. In 1968, Johnson was so concerned that he kept in the White House a large aerial photograph of Khe Sanh with locations of up-to-the-minute positions of American and NVA/VC forces. There was also a model of the Khe Sanh landscape which the President could study.

CIA headquarters reproduced aerial photographs of Dien Bien Phu given to the US by the French. They were sent to Westmoreland's office in Saigon, where he and his staff analyzed them for pertinent

lessons to be applied to Khe Sanh. Westmoreland called Khe Sanh a "vain attempt" by the North Vietnamese "to restage Dien Bien Phu." He insisted throughout his stint as head of MACV that the city attacks of the Tet Offensive were a diversion for attacks against Khe Sanh and other northern regions. He believed he could prevent "another Dien Bien Phu" through use of B-52s and unlimited bombing capability—firepower far beyond anything the French used—as well as better artillery and air mobility. His confidence in US ability to out fire the NVA/VC and his decision to se-

riously defend Khe Sanh was supported by the Joint Chiefs of Staff.

There are other relevant facts about Khe Sanh and Dien Bien Phu which cannot be ignored. First, Dien Bien Phu induced a "final battle" atmosphere for both sides. The French and Vietminh each badly needed a decisive military victory before entering diplomatic talks. The defeat of the French made the French people feel that they had no chance of winning the war and it was no longer worth the steep price they were paying. With the firepower that the Americans possessed in 1968, there was little chance of

Marines watch F-4 drop bombs to clear perimeter at Khe Sanh.

the NVA/VC achieving such a complete military victory that the American people and government would be demoralized enough to stop the war. Also, at Dien Bien Phu, 8,000 Vietminh soldiers and 2,000 French soldiers were killed. Once again, American resources made it unlikely that US troops would suffer such heavy casualties.

General Giap claimed after the Tet Offensive that the battle at Khe Sanh became a major issue due to Americans' fear of lost prominence in the world community. The US believed the French were weakened in that regard by Dien Bien Phu and did not want to take that risk. A former Viet Cong official stated in his memoirs that the Algerian Minister of Culture and Information in the late 1960s related to him that the French collapse had been instrumental in the Algerian struggle for independence. Before Dien Bien Phu, few people believed that the French could be overcome. After the Vietminh victory, Algerians no longer saw the French as invincible.

Forklift drives past rocket damage to Khe Sanh airway.

Marines study the effects of 105mm howitzer fire on perimeter.

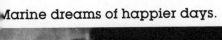

Marine dreams of happier days.

Marine covers his ears during firing stage of artillery attack at Khe Sanh.

TET

Previous page: Wounded VC guerrilla is carried away from the scene of sniper action for interrogation by ARVN soldier.

Above: Infantry platoon patrols Saigon street. Below: APC rolls into Cholon suburb. At right: Troops march through bombed-out section of Cholon suburb.

The perimeter at Khe Sanh shows a maze of sandbags.

Artillery unit provides support fire for perimeter at Khe Sanh. Insets: Marines watch enemy movement from behind sandbags (above) and clean weapons (top right) while waiting for combat activity.

Perimeter defense positions surround camp at Khe Sanh.

Marines conduct search and destroy operation near
DMZ. Tank follows minesweeper. Above: Hut once
used as VC hideout burns.

Rocket attack on Da Nang produces a spectacular sight at night. Opposite left: Sandbags protect Khe Sanh trenches. Opposite right: Sandbags provide perimeter defense. Above: Smoke billows from rocket attack at Khe Sanh.

KHE SANH

DA NANG

At right: Troops inspect cache of weapons taken from VC hideout.

SAIGON

NVA dead litter street after attack on Tan Son Nhut.

VC guerrilla dead remain after embassy attack.

At left: Captured NVA/VC rockets and weapons are displayed. Above: Destroyed C-47 smolders at Tan Son Nhut air base.

At left: Vietnamese search through rubble following battle for Saigon. Below: American troops fight block-by-block in downtown Saigon.

Supplies are air-dropped into Khe Sanh during the siege.

Marines fire a 105mm howitzer during second week of the attack.

Supplies dropped from low-flying C-130s parachute down on pallets.

Marines extend the perimeter by building bunkers with sandbags.

Temporary firing positions line the perimeter at Khe Sanh.

Hills around the base camp at Khe Sanh are pockmarked from constant artillery fire.

Marines recover ammunition dropped from C-130 which missed the drop zone.

Marines contemplate VC mortar attack on Khe Sanh.

An F-4 Phantom jet delivers air strike support during VC mortar attack.

Much-needed supplies arrive daily at Khe Sanh.

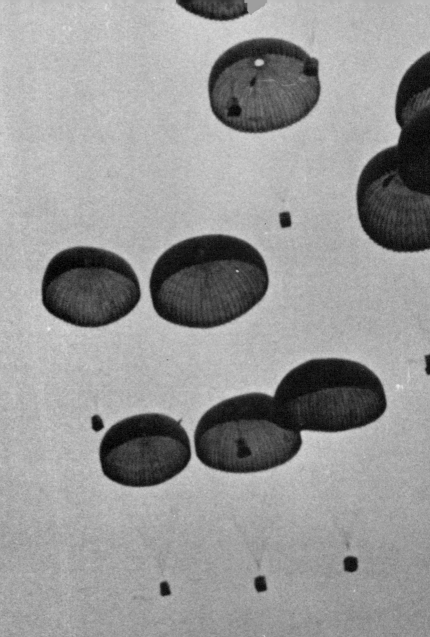

By mid-February, a new delivery system was needed at Khe Sanh. The most common form of delivery was LAPES (Low Altitude Parachute Extraction System), in which entire plane loads of pallets were released when small parachutes triggered the reefing on cargo parachutes.

A disabled 2½ ton truck sits on the perimeter after being hit during VC attack. Inset: LAPES delivery of supplies to base.

At left: Marine demonstrates the proper loading and firing procedure for a 60mm mortar weapon. At right: Interior of C-130 is emptied during LAPES delivery. At right, bottom: C-130 plane is attacked as it attempts a landing to unload supplies. The VC attacks on supply planes were so intense that new delivery systems were devised to bring supplies and ammunition to the Marines at Khe Sanh.

Ground support fire from the perimeter at Khe Sanh included the 105mm howitzer (above), as well as the individual infantryman's M-16 (below). In early February the VC advanced to within 33 feet of the perimeter at Khe Sanh.

The interior lines of the base camp were a labyrinth of underground tunnels.

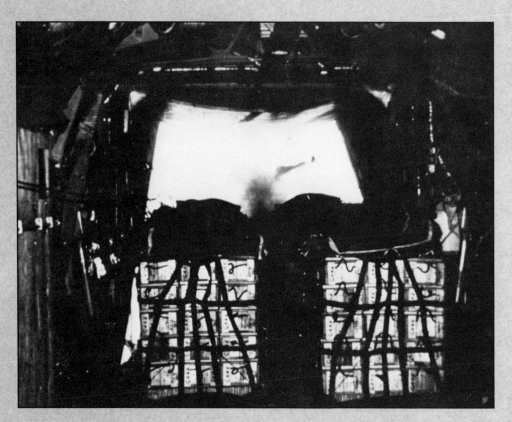

Getting supplies into the Khe Sanh camp was difficult during the three and one-half months of fighting during the Tet Offensive. Air Force pilots were used because of their experience, but the delivery under fire required good weather conditions which never seemed to last more than a few days.

Marines string barbed wire under fire on the perimeter at Khe Sanh.

Marines man M-16 machine gun position on the perimeter. In late February the enemy launched a night attack which was repelled by heavy machine gun fire.

Marine cools down during a break in the action.

On April 1st, Operation Pegasus was launched to rescue the besieged camp at Khe Sanh. Here troops of the 1st Marine Regiment move toward Khe Sanh. Their mission was to reopen Route 9, an important supply route to Khe Sanh.

An M-48 tank and crew sweep a jungle road
for mines as part of the effort to rescue Khe Sanh.

The rough terrain around Khe Sanh was thoroughly checked for possible enemy mines and traps, especially former NVA/VC posts.

On April 8, the relief of Khe Sanh was complete, Route 9 was reopened, and constant vigilance was no longer necessary. The battle for Khe Sanh had lasted 77 days during which time over 75,000 tons of explosives were dropped on enemy positions. After all the enormous effort to defend and rescue the base it was abandoned on June 27, 1968.

View of cemetery at Tan Son Nhut air base shows shacks in foreground.

Who Won?

Judgments regarding the winner of Tet vary with the persons making the judgments. Generally, those using numbers as criteria—mostly American military personnel and some government officials—claim the US and South Vietnam won. The number of NVA/VC casualties was much greater than that of American and South Vietnamese casualties. Also, the North Vietnamese/Viet Cong were unable to hold any city permanently. They remained in Hue and Saigon for more than three weeks, but otherwise, they were driven out of cities within a few days. At the same time, ARVN/USAF troops had plenty of weaponry and air support at their disposal, a factor when monetary values are included in statistics used for gauging a winner.

On the other hand, those people, looking at what events during Tet accomplished, contend that the NVA/VC fared better. To their own benefit, they managed to speed up the war, bringing it into the southern population centers and drawing the attention of Americans in the States. The Tet Offensive convinced some civilians and government officials to reject Johnson's Vietnam policy as unworkable and planted seeds of doubt regarding the policy in many other people's minds. Before the spring of 1968 ended, there were advocates of troop withdrawal within the United States government.

Theories concerning what the NVA/VC intended to accomplish with Tet are numerous. One theory holds that the Tet Offensive was a last-ditch effort on the part of the North Vietnamese to win a major military battle. According to this theory, the NVA/VC wanted to gain control of the government, and considered only military means to achieve this end. They tried to build up their military forces towards such a victory but were thwarted when ARVN/USAF forces implemented counter buildups. American Army leaders could not understand why the NVA/VC would even try to overcome American war technology.

A related theory also assumes that the NVA/VC sought a military victory. Westmoreland contended from the beginning that the NVA/VC's goal was the takeover of Khe Sanh and that the many attacks at Tet were meant as distractions to draw troops from the I Corps base. This theory helps to explain why, relative to the number of Viet Cong involved in the Tet attacks, so few NVA regulars assaulted the cities. The North Vietnamese wanted to concentrate on the logistical goal of Khe Sanh, so they turned over to the South Vietnamese Viet Cong the diversionary assaults on southern urban areas.

Other people said that Westmoreland's theory was backwards. The purpose of the Tet Offensive was not to draw attention away from Khe Sanh; rather, the purpose of the siege at the Marine base was to draw attention away from the attacks in the cities. If Khe Sanh were the main objective, critics of Westmoreland ask, why did the NVA/VC not take better advantage of Khe Sanh's lack of ammunition when they first blew up the ammo dump on January 21. Why did they not keep up a heavier barrage of fire into the base? The Vietminh had used much more firepower at Dien Bien Phu than the NVA/VC used at Khe Sanh. And why did they not sabotage the Khe Sanh water supply? The base's water came from a creek that flowed through the camp, but originated outside the perimeter, easily accessible to the attacking NVA/VC.

By most accounts, the NVA/VC depended on a general uprising among South Vietnamese civilians to augment the existing resistance and to weaken support for South Vietnamese President Thieu. This did not happen. Although most urban civilians did not tell authorities of Viet Cong infiltration, and some Saigon intellectuals joined the resistance after Tet in an effort to get rid of the Americans, few people actively joined the offensive. Only in Hue could any kind of NLF government be established, and that lasted only briefly.

In the minds of NVA/VC leadership, however, US political reaction to the offensive offset losses in most other arenas. Political repercussions in Washington affected the strategy for the rest of the war and helped convince Lyndon Johnson not to seek an-

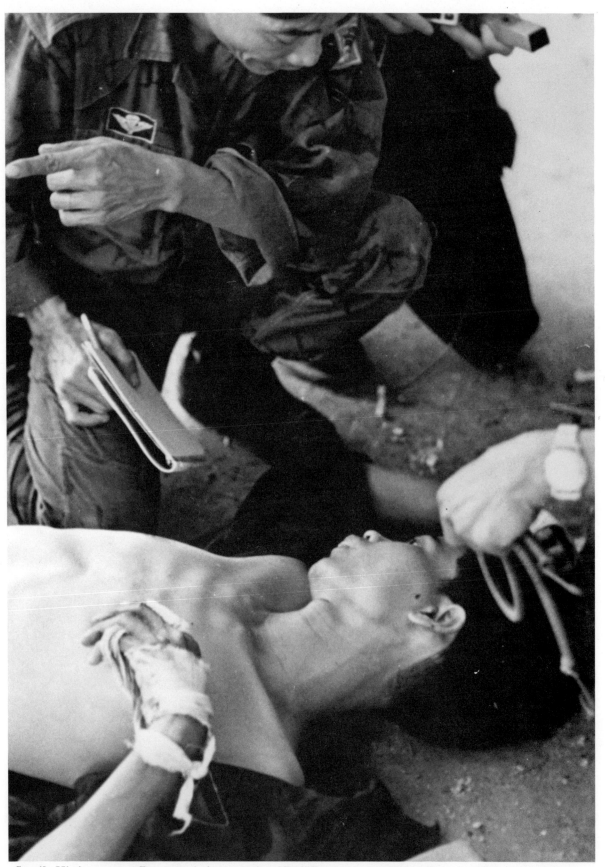

South Vietnamese Ranger interrogates Viet Cong guerrilla at Tan Son Nhut air base.

other term as President.

Many civilians in the States, both in and out of the government, were confused and dismayed by Tet. Westmoreland had assured them that the ARVN/USAF were winning and that the Viet Cong were being routed out of the jungles. That the enemy could so easily wage a strong, nationwide offensive raised doubts in many minds about the effectiveness of American policy regarding Southeast Asia. Most Americans at home believed in the technology and justness of the American way of life. Not only had Westmoreland said the Americans were winning, but by all logic, they ought to have been winning. After more than two years of fighting, American forces should have already won. Defeat by Third World guerrillas was incomprehensible.

As most of the cities attacked during Tet returned to South Vietnamese control, Johnson's extensive pre-Tet worries about whether there were enough troops in Vietnam, and more specifically in Khe Sanh, led to the request for additional troops. Westmoreland received several cables in Saigon from Wheeler indicating the President's concern and intimating that Johnson might approve escalation of ground troops into Laos, Cambodia, and North Vietnam. Taking the hint from General Wheeler, Westmoreland submitted his formal request for troops on February 12. In direct contradiction to the optimistic language he had used previously, Westmoreland now said he "desperately needed" the 525,000 troops he had been promised earlier. McNamara approved deployment of more troops, but the Joint Chiefs refused to recommend it. After the new year's offensive, they said troops at American military bases worldwide were stretched thin because so many soldiers had already been sent to Vietnam. Fresh deployments would entail calling up the reserves. Johnson, however, overrode the chiefs and authorized 10,500 troops to be deployed immediately, without calling up reserve forces.

Johnson sent Wheeler to Vietnam to find out how many more troops would be necessary. Wheeler met with Westmoreland, and

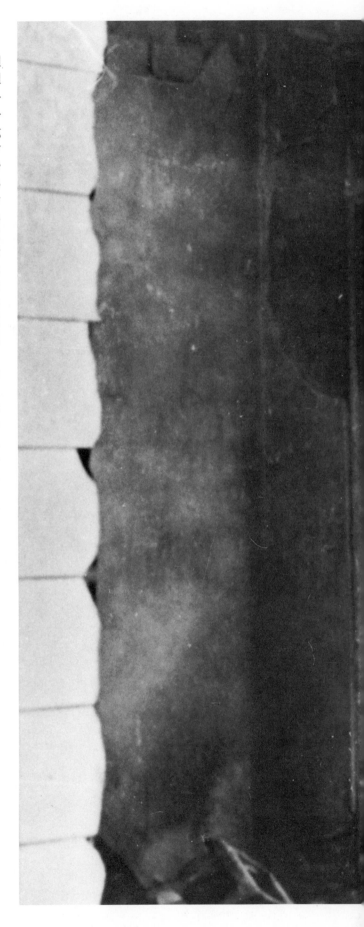

Considerable damage shows on buildings in area of Tan Son Nhut air base.

the two men worked out a strategy which would extend the ground war laterally into Laos and Cambodia. They decided that another 206,000 soldiers would be necessary for such an extension. When Wheeler returned to Washington, however, he said nothing of the new strategy, but only that the enemy would be able to continue fighting for an undetermined length of time. He said 206,000 more troops were needed to protect South Vietnam under the current policy of bombing and ground search-and-destroy missions.

At this point, Johnson asked civilians on his staff for recommendations regarding the troop request. Their criticisms had a great impact.

Johnson thought he was bringing in a supporter for his policies when he asked the elegant, urbane Clark Clifford to replace McNamara as Secretary of Defense. When Johnson asked him for suggestions regarding the request for more troops, Clifford formed a task force to help formulate policy. The intense study of US policy in Vietnam helped to transform this former hawk into a resigned dove.

Although Clifford did not take office until March 1, the task force met on February 28. Assistants in the Defense Department, dismayed by a superior who favored the White House policy, seized the opportunity to re-educate the newcomer. Among the more influential members of the committee were Paul Warnke, Assistant Secretary of Defense for International Security Affairs; Paul Nitze, Deputy Secretary of Defense; and Phil G. Goulding, Assistant Secretary of Defense for Public Affairs—all had helped to convince McNamara of the folly of continuing Johnson's policy in Vietnam. Meetings with his staff and with the task force led Clifford to question the goals of the war, as well as the means. Would the troops which Westmoreland requested help to end the war faster? Would the public stand for such an increase in troop strength? When would the price which Americans were paying in this war become too high? Clifford could find few satisfying answers.

Warnke submitted a memorandum ex-plaining why troop augmentation was impractical and aimless. The memo offered more than an analysis of the policy of the war; it suggested a new strategy to replace the old strategy of attrition, of killing as many North Vietnamese and Viet Cong as possible until the enemy grew tired and gave up. Warnke advised that the American role should be to train ARVN soldiers to become more effective in their own country, to protect urban centers from the type of destruction brought on by Tet, and to try to facilitate peace proceedings.

The Joint Chiefs argued vehemently in defense of their strategy of attrition and bombing at a March 1 meeting attended by Clifford and Warnke, while the military faction of Clifford's task force argued that heavier, extended firepower would bring the war to a close. Due to military arguments against Warnke's stance, a milder version of Warnke's memorandum was given to Johnson on March 4, which recommended the first deployment of 22,000 troops and the calling up of 245,000 reserve soldiers. On a larger scale, it called for a future link between ARVN performance and increase in US troop strength—with subsequent requests for more troops for Southeast Asia, the military would have to demonstrate that ARVN forces were indeed improving. And it opened to the President some of the larger questions regarding the war, something Warnke later said was the primary goal of the Defense Department staff.

Johnson was torn between his civilian advisers and reports from the military. To add to his problems, on March 12, *The New York Times* ran a story disclosing Westmoreland's request for 206,000 troops, implying that Johnson and Westmoreland had not honestly explained the situation regarding American progress in Vietnam to the public, i.e., according to earlier reports Westmoreland should not have needed so many fresh soldiers.

Meanwhile, Johnson's popularity was decreasing steadily, faster than the decrease in approval for the war. Although Johnson was not formally entered in the presidential primaries and so not on the ballot, he was expected to win by a landslide on March 12 in New Hampshire through a write-in campaign. Instead, the little-known Minnesota Senator Eugene McCarthy, campaigning as a peace candidate, won 42.4 percent of the Democratic vote, compared to Johnson's 49.5 percent. Opinion polls showed later that many of those who voted for McCarthy knew little about him or his platform, but wished only to vote against Johnson and his handling of the war. An added irritation in Johnson's political life was the entry of New York Senator Robert Kennedy in the race for Democratic presidential nominee. Johnson had served as John Kennedy's vice-president and had never felt comfortable with Robert Kennedy, who now was also against the war. Robert Kennedy visited Johnson shortly before announcing his candidacy and offered to stay out of the race if Johnson agreed to stop the bombing in North Vietnam. Johnson refused.

Shortly thereafter, members of Congress expressed their displeasure with American progress in Vietnam and called for a review of policy in Southeast Asia. Johnson realized that he had exceeded the limits of his influence in Congress with previous Great Society legislation and knew he would not see any more of his social programs passed. Attempting to serve another term would only hurt the Democratic Party. The economy, too, was suffering from the strain of both increased social spending and the war. And finally, Johnson was aware that his health had been declining since he suffered a heart attack several years earlier.

In late March, Johnson met with his most trusted advisers from both within and outside the government for briefing on the situation in Vietnam and Washington. The culmination occurred on the 25th in a meeting with all of the so-called Wise Men. The majority of those in attendance told him that South Vietnam must play a larger role in its own war and that the US role should be reduced at the same time a peaceful settlement was developed. The consensus differed greatly from earlier meetings in 1967, when only George Ball advocated withdrawal.

For the remainder of the month, Johnson and his speech writers worked on a public statement to be made on the 31st. His message dealt with four issues: the unconditional end to much of the bombing in North Vietnam; the small increase in numbers of troops to go to Vietnam; the efforts to improve ARVN forces; and his decision not to run again for President.

According to polls, Walter Cronkite, anchorman for the CBS Evening News, was the most trusted man in the country. His immediate reaction to Johnson's speech summarized that of most of the country: "What the hell is going on? I thought we were winning the war!" Soon after Tet, Cronkite visited South Vietnam, even staying in Hue as the fighting continued.

On February 27, Cronkite, a former supporter of American policy in Southeast Asia and usually not given to editorializing, presented a special report and ended with his own evaluation of the war. The barometer of American public opinion concluded. ". . . It now seems more certain than ever that the bloody experience in Vietnam is to end a stalemate. . . . it is increasingly clear to this reporter that the only rational way out then will be to negotiate, not as victors but as an honorable people who lived up to their pledge to defend democracy, and did the best they could."

Cache of captured enemy ammunition is
displayed for the press outside Saigon.

Troops patrol streets near Tan Son Nhut air base in early May 1968.

At left: **Captured NVA/VC weapons are shown to ARVN troops.** Above:
Soldier fires M-16 to dislodge sniper in Cholon suburb.

Troops of the 9th Infantry Division advance through the rubble south of the ''Y'' bridge in Saigon.

Above: **Troops march through bombed-out streets near the Kinh Poi Canal district of Saigon.** At right: **Infantry soldiers run for cover during air support strike in Saigon.** Below: **NVA Regulars lie dead in the street following their abortive attempt to liberate Saigon.**